The Prepper's Ultimate Guide: Building Sustainable Shelters for Long-Term Survival

Lloyd Green

Published by Lloyd Green, 2023.

While every precaution has been taken in the preparation of this book, the publisher assumes no responsibility for errors or omissions, or for damages resulting from the use of the information contained herein.

THE PREPPER'S ULTIMATE GUIDE: BUILDING SUSTAINABLE SHELTERS FOR LONG-TERM SURVIVAL

First edition. October 16, 2023.

ISBN: 979-8223268420

Written by Lloyd Green.

Also by Lloyd Green

The Prepper's Ultimate Guide: Building Sustainable Shelters for Long-Term Survival

Original Six Era: The Rise of the Chicago Blackhawks Dynasty

Table of Contents

The Prepper's Ultimate Guide: Building Sustainable Shelters for Long-Term Survival

Explore eco-friendly shelter-building techniques, including renewable energy sources, rainwater collection systems, and sustainable materials for long-term survival

Types of Sustainable Shelters for Preppers

1. Earth Sheltered Homes: These underground or partially underground homes offer natural insulation and protection from extreme weather conditions. Constructed with the surrounding earth acting as a barrier, these shelters reduce energy consumption by regulating temperature efficiently.

2. Straw Bale Houses: These structures use straw bales for insulation, which are inexpensive and eco-friendly. The thick walls provide excellent insulation properties while allowing for easy construction and customization.

3. Shipping Container Homes: Repurposing shipping containers into living spaces is becoming increasingly popular among preppers due to their durability and affordability. With proper modifications, these containers can be transformed into comfortable and sustainable dwellings that withstand harsh conditions.

Location and Site Selection for Long-Term Survival

When it comes to long-term survival, the location and site selection of your shelter is crucial. Here are some important factors to consider:

- **Proximity to water sources**: Find a location near a clean and reliable water source, such as a river or well. Water is essential for survival, so ensure easy access.

- **Climate conditions**: Consider the climate in your chosen area. Extreme temperatures or frequent natural disasters might make survival more challenging.

- **Terrain features**: Look for flat or slightly elevated ground that will allow proper drainage and prevent flooding. Avoid areas prone to landslides or avalanches.

- **Availability of natural resources**: Choose an area with abundant natural resources like forests for firewood, hunting grounds for food, and materials for building shelters.

Remember that the ultimate goal is sustainability - choose a location that offers long-term viability and can support you self-sufficiently over time.

Essential Tools and Materials for Shelter Construction

To successfully build a sustainable shelter for long-term survival, it is crucial to have the right tools and materials. Here are some essentials:

- **Hand Tools:** Basic hand tools such as hammers, saws, axes, shovels, and utility knives are indispensable. They allow you to cut wood, dig holes, shape materials, and assemble your shelter.

- **Building Materials:** Gathering building materials in advance can save you valuable time during an emergency situation. You will need sturdy items like lumber or logs for framing your structure. Don't forget about waterproofing materials like tarps or plastic sheets that offer protection from rain.

- **Fasteners and Adhesives:** Nails, screws, bolts, zip ties - having plenty of fasteners on hand will ensure structural integrity during construction. Additionally, adhesives like glue or epoxy can hold smaller components together securely.

By stocking up on these tools and materials beforehand and familiarizing yourself with their use through practice projects or online guides at an appropriate reading level, you will be well-prepared to construct a reliable shelter that can withstand the challenges of long-term survival situations.

Designing a Resilient Shelter for Survival Scenarios

In survival scenarios, having a resilient shelter is crucial for long-term sustainability. Here are some key considerations to keep in mind when designing your shelter:

- **Location:** Choose a location that is well-protected and hidden from potential threats. Look for areas with natural barriers like hills, dense vegetation, or rocky terrain.

- **Durability:** Invest in sturdy materials like reinforced concrete or thick timber to ensure your shelter can withstand harsh weather conditions and physical impacts.

- **Energy Efficiency:** Implement energy-saving features such as insulation, solar panels, and efficient heating systems to reduce reliance on external energy sources.

- **Water Management:** Install rainwater collection systems and filters to ensure a steady supply of clean water. Consider digging wells or constructing underground cisterns for additional storage capacity.

By prioritizing these factors in the design of your shelter, you can increase your chances of long-term survival during challenging times. Remember that adaptability and resourcefulness are equally important – be prepared to modify and innovate as needed.

Building Techniques for Eco-Friendly Shelters

When it comes to building sustainable shelters for long-term survival, there are a few key techniques that preppers should consider. These methods not only minimize the impact on the environment but also promote self-sufficiency and resilience in challenging scenarios.

One effective technique is using natural and locally sourced materials. By utilizing materials such as wood, straw, clay, or stone from nearby areas, preppers can reduce their carbon footprint and support local economies. Additionally, these natural materials often have excellent insulation properties, which can help maintain a comfortable temperature inside the shelter without relying heavily on external energy sources.

Another important consideration is passive design principles. By incorporating features like proper orientation, ventilation systems, and shading devices into the shelter's design, preppers can maximize energy efficiency while minimizing dependence on artificial heating or cooling systems. This not only saves resources but also ensures a more comfortable living environment even during extreme weather conditions.

Furthermore,

- Rainwater harvesting systems can be installed to collect and store water for various uses.

- The use of renewable energy sources such as solar panels or small wind turbines helps meet power needs sustainably.

- Composting toilets minimize waste output while enriching soil fertility.

By employing these building techniques for eco-friendly shelters, preppers can create resilient living spaces that prioritize both their own well-being and the health of our planet.

Incorporating Renewable Energy Sources in Your Shelter

When building a sustainable shelter for long-term survival, incorporating renewable energy sources is essential. Here are some key options to consider:

1. Solar power: Install solar panels on the roof of your shelter to harness the sun's energy and convert it into electricity. This is a reliable and eco-friendly solution that can provide consistent power for various needs.
2. Wind turbines: If you live in an area with strong winds, consider adding a small wind turbine to generate electricity. It can be especially useful during stormy weather or when sunlight is limited.
3. Micro-hydro system: If you have access to running water nearby, such as a stream or river, explore the possibility of setting up a micro-hydro system. This uses the gravitational force of flowing water to produce clean energy.

By incorporating these renewable energy sources into your shelter design, you can reduce reliance on non-renewable resources and ensure long-term sustainability for your survival needs.

Harnessing Solar Power for Sustainable Living

Solar power is a key component of sustainable living. By harnessing the sun's energy, preppers can ensure long-term survival in their shelters. Installing solar panels on the roof or around the shelter allows for the capture of sunlight and conversion into electricity.

Benefits of solar power include its renewable nature, making it a reliable source even during extended emergencies. The upfront cost may be high, but the potential savings on utility bills in the long run outweighs this initial investment. Additionally, solar power reduces reliance on fossil fuels, which helps to combat climate change.

To maximize efficiency, it is important to position solar panels where they receive optimal exposure to sunlight throughout the day. This requires careful planning and strategic placement based on factors such as shade from trees or nearby structures.

Investing in batteries is also crucial as they store excess energy generated by solar panels for use during nighttime or cloudy days when sunlight may be insufficient. Battery management systems are available that help monitor and regulate energy storage levels effectively.

Overall, incorporating solar power into sustainable shelters offers numerous benefits including decreased reliance on traditional power sources and reduced carbon footprint.

Utilizing Wind Power for Off-Grid Shelter Solutions

Harnessing the power of wind can provide a sustainable and reliable energy source for off-grid shelter solutions. By installing wind turbines, preppers can generate electricity even in remote locations, ensuring their long-term survival.

Benefits of Wind Power:

- Independence: With wind power, preppers aren't reliant on traditional electrical grids that may fail during emergencies or be unavailable in remote areas.

- Cost-effective: Once the initial setup costs are covered, wind power is virtually free as it relies on an abundant natural resource.

- Sustainability: Unlike fossil fuels which contribute to climate change, harnessing wind power helps reduce greenhouse gas emissions and promotes environmental stewardship.

Considerations for Implementing Wind Power:

1. Site selection: It's essential to choose a location with consistent and strong winds to maximize energy production. Conduct thorough research or seek expert advice before installation.
2. Equipment efficiency: Investing in high-quality turbines ensures optimal performance and durability over time.
3. Maintenance routine: Regular inspections and maintenance will prevent issues such as wear and tear from impacting

system efficiency.

By incorporating wind power into off-grid shelters, preppers can enjoy the benefits of renewable energy while preparing for any long-term survival scenario.

Hydroelectric Power Generation for Self-Sufficiency

Hydroelectric power is a reliable and sustainable energy source that can provide self-sufficiency for long-term survival. With the right setup, you can harness the power of water to generate electricity without relying on external sources. Here are some key points to consider:

- **Water as an Energy Source**: Water possesses immense kinetic energy that can be harnessed using turbines connected to generators. By utilizing a flowing stream or even building your own small dam, you can tap into this natural resource.

- **Powering Shelters**: Hydroelectric power generation allows you to keep essential appliances running during emergencies. This includes heating systems, refrigeration units, communication devices, and lighting fixtures – all crucial for maintaining comfort and security in your sustainable shelter.

- **Sustainable Alternative**: Unlike fossil fuel-based generators or solar panels dependent on sunlight availability, hydroelectric systems have the advantage of operating continuously as long as water flows steadily. Installing such a system ensures uninterrupted access to electricity regardless of weather conditions or fuel supplies.

By incorporating hydroelectric power generation into your sustainable shelter plans, you take important steps toward achieving independence and resilience in the face of extended periods without grid electricity.

Rainwater Collection and Purification Systems

Rainwater collection and purification systems are essential for long-term survival in sustainable shelters.

- **Collecting rainwater** involves setting up a system to capture rainfall from roofs or other surfaces and store it in containers or tanks. This water can be used for various purposes such as drinking, cooking, cleaning, and gardening.

- When collecting rainwater, it is important to ensure the **adequate filtration** of the water. Filtration systems remove debris, sediment, and contaminants that may be present in the collected rainwater.

- To further enhance the quality of collected rainwater, **purification methods** can be employed. These methods include boiling the water to kill bacteria and parasites or using chemical disinfectants like chlorine.

Having a reliable rainwater collection system ensures a constant supply of clean water even during extended periods without access to traditional sources. It forms an integral part of building resilient shelter structures suitable for long-term survival scenarios.

Sustainable Heating and Cooling Options for Shelters

When it comes to ensuring a comfortable and sustainable living environment in your shelter for long-term survival, it's essential to consider heating and cooling options. Here are a few energy-efficient solutions:

1. Passive solar design: Incorporating passive solar elements into the architecture of your shelter can dramatically reduce the need for artificial heating and cooling. By strategically positioning windows, insulation, and thermal mass materials like concrete or stone, you can maximize natural heat gain during winter months while minimizing excessive heat buildup in summer.
2. Solar panels: Installing solar panels on the roof of your shelter allows you to harness renewable energy from the sun. This electricity can power efficient electric heaters or air conditioners, reducing reliance on fossil fuels.
3. Geothermal systems: Utilizing the consistent temperature underground, geothermal systems can efficiently heat or cool your shelter throughout the year by exchanging heat between underground pipes and your home's HVAC system.

By considering these sustainable heating and cooling options when building your long-term survival shelters, not only will you be prepared for any situation but also contribute towards a greener future with reduced environmental impact.

Natural Ventilation and Insulation Methods

Natural Ventilation Methods

- Utilize cross ventilation by placing windows or vents on opposite sides of the shelter to allow for airflow.

- Install adjustable louvers on windows or vents so that you can control the amount of air coming in.

- Consider using solar-powered fans to enhance natural airflow and circulation within the shelter.

Insulation Methods

- Use eco-friendly insulation materials such as cellulose, wool, or straw bales, which not only provide thermal insulation but also reduce environmental impact.

- Seal any gaps or cracks in the walls and floors to prevent heat loss or gain.

- Incorporate double-glazed windows and doors with weatherstripping for enhanced insulation.

Composting Toilets and Waste Management in Shelters

Composting Toilets for Sustainable Waste Management in Shelters

Composting toilets are a sustainable solution for waste management in long-term survival shelters.

- These toilets function by decomposing human waste into nutrient-rich compost that can be safely used as fertilizer.

- They use little to no water, making them ideal for situations where water resources are scarce or limited.

- Composting toilets also help reduce the spread of harmful pathogens commonly associated with traditional flush toilets.

Benefits and Considerations of Composting Toilets

There are several benefits and considerations to keep in mind when using composting toilets in shelters:

- Environmentally friendly: Composting toilets eliminate the need for septic tanks, reducing pollution and strain on natural resources.

- Cost-effective: With minimal maintenance requirements, these systems prove to be cost-effective over time.

- Odor control: Proper ventilation ensures odor-free operation, creating a comfortable living environment within the shelter. However, it's important to note that these systems require regular monitoring and proper management to ensure they work effectively. Without proper maintenance, there is a risk of odor buildup or incomplete decomposition.

Growing Food Indoors: Hydroponics and Aquaponics

Hydroponics and aquaponics offer effective solutions for growing food indoors, making them ideal options for long-term survival scenarios.

In hydroponic systems, plants are grown in nutrient-rich water without soil, using a variety of methods such as nutrient film technique (NFT), deep water culture (DWC), or wick systems. These systems require careful monitoring of pH levels, nutrients, and water temperature to ensure optimal plant growth.

Aquaponics takes hydroponic farming one step further by combining it with aquaculture. Fish waste provides the necessary nutrients for the plants while the plants filter out toxins from the water—creating a symbiotic relationship between fish and plants. The result is two sustainable sources of food in one system: fresh produce and protein from fish.

Both hydroponic and aquaponic setups can be customized to fit any space - whether it's a basement or a small room within your shelter. They also allow you to grow crops year-round regardless of external weather conditions - ensuring a consistent supply of nutritious food even during long-term emergencies.

Here are some benefits:

- Efficient use of resources: Both hydroponic and aquaponic systems minimize water usage compared to traditional soil-based farming.

- Faster growth rates: Plants grown through these methods often mature faster than their counterparts cultivated outdoors.

- Greater control over environmental factors: You have complete control over lighting intensity, temperature, humidity levels etc., allowing you to optimize plant growth.

- Higher crop yields per square foot: By eliminating competition with weeds & optimizing growing conditions indoors; both these methods lead to higher crop yield per unit area.

Whether you choose hydroponics or aquaponics depends on your specific needs but both techniques provide an excellent means of producing nutritious food in limited spaces — perfect for preppers looking for sustainable solutions during extended stays in their shelters.

Creating Sustainable Water Sources for Long-Term Survival

Water is essential for human survival, and ensuring a sustainable water source is crucial when preparing for long-term survival. Here are some strategies to consider:

1. **Rainwater Harvesting**: Install rain barrels or a larger cistern to collect rainwater from rooftops. This can provide a reliable supply of water during the rainy seasons.
2. **Well Digging**: If you have access to suitable land, consider digging a well. It can provide a consistent source of groundwater that won't rely on external factors like rainfall.
3. **Water Filtration and Purification**: Invest in high-quality water filtration systems or portable purification devices such as chlorine tablets or UV sterilizers. These will eliminate harmful bacteria, viruses, and contaminants from any water sources you come across.

Remember, having multiple backup options for obtaining clean drinking water is vital in case one fails. By implementing these strategies, you increase your chances of accessing potable water and ensuring your long-term survival plan remains intact even in challenging circumstances.

Securing and Reinforcing Your Shelter for Safety

Ensure strong foundation and structural integrity

- Before building your shelter, make sure you have a solid and level foundation to prevent structural weaknesses.

- Use high-quality building materials such as concrete or reinforced steel to ensure the durability of your shelter.

- Regularly inspect your shelter for any signs of damage or wear that could compromise its stability.

Reinforce doors and windows

- Install sturdy locks on all entry points of your shelter to prevent unauthorized access.

- Consider reinforcing doors with metal plates or installing security bars on windows to deter potential intruders.

- Seal any gaps around doors and windows to keep out drafts, insects, and small animals.

Create a defensive perimeter

- Surround your shelter with natural barriers like thorny bushes or fences to discourage trespassers.

- Implement early warning systems such as tripwires or motion sensor lights to alert you of approaching threats.

- Establish clear communication channels with nearby neighbors or fellow preppers for assistance during emergencies.

Shelter Maintenance and Repairs in Survival Situations

Regular maintenance and prompt repairs are essential for ensuring the long-term durability of your shelter. Here are a few key considerations to keep in mind:

1. **Inspect all structural elements:** Conduct regular inspections, paying close attention to the walls, roof, and foundation of your shelter. Look out for any signs of damage or wear that could compromise its integrity.
2. **Address leaks promptly:** A leaky shelter can lead to dampness and mold growth, making it uncomfortable and potentially hazardous for long-term survival. Seal any cracks or gaps immediately using waterproof materials such as caulk or sealant.
3. **Maintain cleanliness:** Regularly clean both the interior and exterior of your shelter to prevent the buildup of dirt, debris, pests, and allergens that could impact air quality.

Addressing Fire Safety in Sustainable Shelters

When building sustainable shelters for long-term survival, it is crucial to prioritize fire safety. Here are some key points to consider:

- **Fire-resistant materials:** Choose materials that have a high resistance to fire, such as concrete or stone, for the construction of your shelter. Avoid using flammable materials like wood, which can easily catch fire and spread quickly.

- **Proper ventilation:** Adequate ventilation is essential to prevent the buildup of smoke and toxic gases in case of a fire. Install well-designed ventilation systems that allow for air circulation while minimizing the risk of embers entering the shelter.

- **Smoke detectors and extinguishers:** Equip your shelter with smoke detectors strategically placed throughout the space. Additionally, provide readily accessible firefighting equipment like fire extinguishers at multiple locations within the shelter.

With these precautions in place, you can significantly reduce the risk of fires in your sustainable shelter and ensure the safety of everyone inside. Remember to regularly inspect and maintain all fire safety measures to keep them functional and effective over time.

Building a Community: Sustainable Shelter Sharing

In times of crisis, it is essential to come together as a community and support one another. One way to ensure long-term survival is by sharing sustainable shelters. By collaborating with others, you can divide the workload and pool resources for everyone's benefit.

Here are some key points to remember:

- **Safety in numbers**: When building sustainable shelters, it's beneficial to have multiple pairs of hands working together. Working cooperatively not only reduces individual workloads but also increases safety during construction.

- **Pooling resources**: Sharing shelter-building supplies such as tools, materials, and knowledge can help save costs and increase overall efficiency.

- **Creating bonds**: Collaborating on building projects fosters a sense of community and builds strong relationships among individuals who might otherwise be strangers.

By establishing cooperative living arrangements within your community, you not only increase your chances for survival but also create an environment where individuals can thrive together.

Long-Term Survival Strategies for Sustainable Shelters

Design for Energy Efficiency

- When building a sustainable shelter for long-term survival, it is crucial to prioritize energy efficiency. This means incorporating design elements that minimize the need for heating or cooling and maximize natural lighting. Proper insulation, well-sealed windows, and efficient thermal mass can all contribute to reducing energy consumption.

- Utilizing passive solar design techniques can further enhance the energy efficiency of your sustainable shelter. Positioning windows towards the sun's path allows for maximum heat gain in winter while shading them during summer prevents overheating. This strategic placement helps maintain a comfortable temperature inside without relying heavily on mechanical systems.

Harness Renewable Energy Sources

- To ensure long-term sustainability, consider harnessing renewable energy sources within your shelter design. Install solar panels on the roof or strategic locations where they can absorb sunlight throughout the day, generating electricity to power essential appliances and lights.

- Additionally, integrating wind turbines into your sustainable shelter's architecture can provide an alternative source of clean energy when sunlight is limited. By combining solar and wind power systems with battery storage solutions, you create a reliable off-grid setup capable of providing sustained electricity even during emergencies or extended periods without access to public utilities."

Unleashing Creativity: DIY Shelter Construction with Everyday Materials

Showcase creative shelter-building projects using readily available materials like PVC pipes, shipping containers, and salvaged wood.

The Power of Imagination: Unleashing Your Creative Potential

- **Unlocking the mind:** Imagination is a powerful tool that allows us to visualize and create something out of nothing. By tapping into our imagination, we can come up with innovative solutions for shelter construction using everyday materials.

- **Thinking outside the box:** When faced with limited resources, it's crucial to think creatively and explore unconventional ideas. Imagination encourages us to look beyond what already exists and discover new possibilities.

- **Turning constraints into opportunities:** Instead of viewing limitations as obstacles, we can use our imagination to see them as opportunities for innovation. By reframing challenges as creative puzzles, we can find unique ways to build shelters with readily available materials.

- **Breaking free from conventions:** Imagination liberates us from conventional thinking and opens doors to endless possibilities. It allows us to challenge norms, experiment with different concepts, and push boundaries in shelter construction.

- **Inspiring others:** Our imaginative designs have the potential not only to meet practical needs but also inspire others in their own creativity journeys. Sharing our unique DIY shelter constructions may ignite sparks of imagination in those looking for similar solutions.

In conclusion, harnessing the power of imagination is essential when undertaking DIY shelter constructions with everyday materials. It enables us to visualize possibilities beyond what currently exists, turn limitations into opportunities for innovation, break free from conventional thinking patterns, and inspire others along the way. Let your creativity soar by unleashing your imaginative potential today!

DIY Shelter Construction: A Sustainable Solution for All

Building Sustainable Shelters

Constructing DIY shelters using everyday materials provides a sustainable solution for individuals and communities in need. By repurposing common items such as shipping containers, pallets, or discarded building materials, anyone can create durable and functional structures that meet their basic housing needs.

Advantages of DIY Shelter Construction

1. Cost-effective: Utilizing readily available materials significantly reduces the financial burden associated with traditional construction methods.
2. Adaptability: DIY shelter projects allow for flexibility in design and layout to suit individual preferences and specific geographic conditions.
3. Environmental impact: By recycling materials that would otherwise end up in landfills, DIY shelters present an eco-friendly alternative to conventional building practices.
4. Empowerment: Engaging in shelter construction empowers individuals to take control of their living situations while fostering creativity and self-sufficiency.

With a little ingenuity and resourcefulness, constructing sustainable shelters becomes accessible even to those on a limited budget or facing challenging circumstances. Embracing the ethos of "reduce, reuse, recycle," these innovative initiatives contribute positively to both people's lives and the environment at large.

Exploring Unconventional Materials: PVC Pipes and their Versatility

PVC Pipes: A Versatile Construction Material

When it comes to DIY shelter construction, PVC pipes are an unconventional material that offers endless possibilities. These lightweight and durable pipes are known for their versatility, making them a go-to choice for creative builders. From simple structures like tents and awnings to more complex designs such as geodesic domes and greenhouses, the flexibility of PVC pipes allows you to unleash your creativity and construct shelters suitable for various needs.

Advantages of Using PVC Pipes

1. **Affordability**: One of the main advantages of using PVC pipes is their cost-effectiveness. Compared to traditional building materials such as wood or metal, PVC pipes are remarkably inexpensive, making them ideal for budget-conscious DIY enthusiasts.
2. **Ease of Use**: Constructing with PVC pipes requires no advanced technical skills or specialized tools. The simplicity of connecting these pipes through fittings allows even beginners to create sturdy structures with ease.
3. **Durability**: Despite being lightweight, PVC pipes offer impressive durability against harsh weather conditions and general wear and tear. Resistant to rusting, rotting, and degradation from sunlight exposure, they ensure that your shelter remains intact in the long run.
4. **Customizability**: With a wide range of sizes available on the market, you can easily find the perfect dimensions for your project's requirements. Additionally, since PVC can be cut

into specific lengths without compromising its structural integrity, you have complete control over tailoring your design according to your needs.

By harnessing the potential of this unconventional material in crafting shelters creatively suited for different purposes—from emergency housing solutions during natural disasters to makeshift outdoor hangouts—a world of possibilities opens up when working with versatile PVC pipes.

From Trash to Treasure: Salvaged Wood for Eco-Friendly Shelters

- Sustainable Solution: By repurposing salvaged wood, you can create eco-friendly shelters that reduce waste and minimize environmental impact. Instead of contributing to deforestation or relying on new materials, consider using reclaimed wood for your DIY construction projects.

- Abundant Resource: Salvaged wood can be found in various places such as old buildings, barns, or shipping pallets. With a bit of creativity and resourcefulness, you can turn discarded materials into functional and aesthetically pleasing structures. By giving new life to these forgotten pieces of lumber, you not only save money but also give back to the environment by reducing landfill waste.

- Versatile Applications: From flooring to wall panels and furniture pieces, salvaged wood offers endless possibilities for shelter construction. Its weathered appearance adds character while providing durability. Whether it's rustic cabins or modern tiny houses you're dreaming of building, utilizing salvaged wood allows you to unleash your creativity without compromising sustainability principles

Thinking Outside the Box: Innovative Uses for Shipping Containers

Innovative Uses for Shipping Containers

Shipping containers are often seen as simply a means to transport goods across the globe. However, with a little creativity, these sturdy structures can be transformed into unique and functional living spaces.

- **Tiny Homes**: With their compact size and modular design, shipping containers make excellent building blocks for tiny homes. By combining multiple containers or cutting holes for windows and doors, individuals can create stylish and cost-effective dwellings.

- **Offices**: Need an office space in a hurry? Look no further than a shipping container! These versatile structures can be easily converted into comfortable workspaces complete with insulation, electricity, and plumbing.

- **Retail Spaces**: Entrepreneurs on a budget can turn shipping containers into trendy pop-up shops or small boutiques. With some clever interior design techniques and eye-catching displays, these repurposed containers can become attractive retail spaces.

The possibilities are endless when it comes to using shipping containers creatively – all that's needed is some outside-the-box thinking. Whether you're dreaming of a unique home or looking for an innovative business solution, consider harnessing the potential of these everyday materials.

Building on a Budget: Cost-Effective DIY Shelter Solutions

Cost-Effective DIY Shelter Solutions

Looking to build a shelter on a budget? We've got you covered! With some creativity and everyday materials, you can construct your own DIY shelter without breaking the bank. Here are a few cost-effective solutions to consider:

1. Pallets and Tarps

   ○ Pallets can serve as a sturdy base for your shelter.

   ○ Utilize tarps or heavy-duty plastic sheets to provide waterproofing and protection from the elements.

   ○ Secure the tarps to the pallets with zip ties or bungee cords.

2. Straw Bales

   ○ Straw bales are an affordable option that provides great insulation.

   ○ Stack straw bales in layers, leaving enough space for doorways and windows.

   ○ Cover the sides with tarps or other weather-resistant materials.

3. Shipping Containers

○ Repurposing shipping containers is an innovative way to create a budget-friendly shelter.

○ Look for used shipping containers that are still structurally sound.

○ Modify them by adding windows, doors, insulation, and utilities like plumbing and electricity.

These DIY shelter solutions demonstrate how ingenuity can transform everyday materials into functional structures while saving money. By taking advantage of resources readily available, anyone can embrace their creative side and build their dream shelter without breaking the bank.

The Basics of Shelter Design: Key Considerations and Principles

Key Considerations for Shelter Design

When designing a shelter with everyday materials, there are several key considerations to keep in mind.

1. **Functionality**: The shelter should serve its purpose effectively, providing protection from the elements and creating a comfortable living space.
2. **Durability**: Using sturdy materials and construction techniques will ensure that the shelter can withstand various weather conditions and last for an extended period.
3. **Cost-effectiveness**: Opting for affordable or repurposed materials will help keep costs down while still achieving a functional design.

Principles of Shelter Design

To create an effective DIY shelter, it is essential to apply certain design principles:

1. **Optimal Space Utilization**: Maximizing the use of available space is crucial, especially when working with limited resources. Consider using modular or multi-functional furniture and storage solutions to make the most of every square foot.
2. **Insulation and Ventilation**: Proper insulation will regulate temperature inside the shelter, keeping it warm in colder climates and cool in hotter regions. Additionally, strategic ventilation helps maintain air quality by allowing fresh air circulation.

3. **Accessibility**: Allowing easy access into and around the
    shelter ensures convenience for residents with limited
    mobility or disabilities.

Remember these considerations and principles as you embark on your
DIY shelter project, utilizing creativity alongside everyday materials
to construct a practical haven suitable for anyone seeking refuge or
adventure outdoors!

Tools of the Trade: Essential Equipment for DIY Shelter Construction

Essential Equipment for DIY Shelter Construction

Whether you are building a backyard fort or creating a temporary structure for camping, having the right tools is crucial. Here are some essential equipment that will help unleash your creativity in DIY shelter construction:

- **Hammer**: This tool is a must-have for any construction project. It allows you to securely fasten materials together and drive nails into wood.

- **Saw**: A saw is necessary for cutting lumber or branches to the desired lengths. Choose one with sharp teeth and sturdy construction.

When working on your DIY shelter, it's also important to have these additional tools handy:

- **Drill**: A drill comes in handy when assembling structures using screws rather than nails. It can speed up the process significantly and produce more secure connections.

- **Measuring tape**: Accurate measurements are crucial in ensuring that all pieces fit properly together. Use a measuring tape to determine dimensions and make precise cuts.

With these basic tools at your disposal, you'll be well-equipped to construct the perfect homemade shelter using everyday materials

Step-by-Step Guide: Constructing a PVC Pipe Greenhouse

Materials Needed:

- PVC pipes

- Connectors (elbow, T-shaped)

- Plastic sheeting

- Duct tape

- Scissors

- Measuring tape or ruler

Instructions:

1. Measure and mark the dimensions of your greenhouse on the ground using measuring tape or a ruler.
2. Cut the PVC pipes to match the length and height measurements you marked.
3. Assemble the cut pieces of PVC pipe using connectors to create the frame for your greenhouse structure. Use elbow connectors for corner joints and T-shaped connectors for intersections.
4. Attach plastic sheeting to cover each side of the PVC pipe frame, leaving enough excess material to secure at all sides.
5. Securely attach the plastic sheeting to each side of the frame using duct tape or any other strong adhesive, making sure there are no gaps or loose areas that could allow air leaks.
6. Complete assembling all sides of your greenhouse with

attached plastic sheeting until it forms an enclosed structure.

7. Optional: Add additional support by adding extra crosspieces along the horizontal sections if desired, ensuring stability during extreme weather conditions.

8. Create an entrance/exit point by cutting one section of plastic from door-sized opening towards one end and securing with hinges so it opens like a door.

Transforming Salvaged Wood into a Cozy Cabin Retreat

Looking to create your own rustic cabin getaway? Look no further than salvaged wood for all the materials you need. By repurposing old lumber, you can transform it into a warm and inviting space for relaxation.

Here are some simple steps to get you started on your DIY cabin project:

1. **Source Your Materials**: Begin by hunting for salvaged wood in yard sales, construction sites, or even online marketplaces. Keep an eye out for weathered boards with unique textures and patterns that will add character to your cabin.
2. **Prepare the Wood**: Before using salvaged wood, make sure to clean off any dirt or debris. Sand down rough edges and remove any nails or staples from the planks.
3. **Design your Space**: Plan out the layout of your cabin, taking care to consider windows placement for optimal natural light and ventilation. Sketch out a blueprint before you begin construction.
4. **Build Your Frame**: Utilize sturdy salvaged beams as support structures for walls, roof, and floorings. Measure carefully and cut the wood according to your design dimensions.
5. **Add Insulation**: Enhance thermal efficiency by adding insulation between wall studs and under floors using eco-friendly insulation materials like recycled denim or cellulose fiber.
6. **Finish Touches**: Decorate your cozy retreat with reclaimed furniture pieces like repurposed wooden crates converted into shelves or tables. Bring warmth through soft furnishings

such as blankets made from upcycled textiles.

7 **Unleash Creativity Time:** Turn scrap metal into functional items such as hooks, racks, or organizers. Add quirky accessories made from found objects

- think driftwood sculptures or birch bark picture frames. Weave natural elements throughout

- use dried flowers & branches as decorations

With patience, creativity, and resourcefulness, you can turn unwanted salvaged wood into a one-of-a-kind cabin that is both sustainable and charming. Enjoy the satisfaction of creating your perfect retreat while reducing waste and showcasing your craftsmanship skills.

Creative Adaptations: Turning Shipping Containers into Livable Spaces

Affordable and Sustainable Housing Solutions

Shipping containers have become a popular choice for creative individuals seeking affordable and sustainable housing solutions. By repurposing these sturdy steel structures, they can be transformed into functional and livable spaces. With their modular design, shipping containers offer endless possibilities for customization, making them ideal choices for DIY shelter construction projects.

Versatile Design Possibilities

Shipping container homes are incredibly versatile, allowing homeowners to unleash their creativity in designing unique living spaces. The interior layout can be customized according to individual preferences with options ranging from single- or multi-level designs to open-plan concepts or divided rooms. In addition, features like windows, doors, insulation materials, plumbing systems, and electrical wiring can all be easily incorporated into the container's framework.

Advantages of Container Homes

Apart from providing an avenue for self-expression and innovative design ideas using everyday materials like shipping containers as building blocks also present various advantages:

- **Affordability**: Building a shipping container home is often more cost-effective than traditional construction methods.

- **Durability**: Made from durable steel material designed to withstand transportation across oceans means that these structures are highly resistant against harsh weather conditions.

- **Sustainability**: By turning unused shipping containers into livable spaces instead of letting them go to waste in landfills promotes sustainability efforts by reducing carbon footprint through recycling efforts.

Overall, converting ordinary shipping containers into habitable dwellings showcases the potential for creative problem-solving by utilizing readily available resources while also addressing pressing issues such as affordable housing and environmental sustainability

Harnessing Nature's Resources: Incorporating Natural Elements in Shelter Design

Incorporating natural elements into shelter design can enhance both the aesthetic appeal and functionality of a DIY shelter. By harnessing nature's resources, you can create a sustainable and eco-friendly structure that blends seamlessly with its surroundings.

- **Using plants:** Integrating living plants into the design adds not only beauty but also improves air quality and provides shade. Consider using climbing vines to cover walls or roofs for natural insulation and privacy. Select native plant species, as they are better adapted to local conditions and require less maintenance.

- **Maximizing natural light:** Effective use of windows, skylights, or solar tubes can fill your shelter with ample natural light during the day, reducing reliance on artificial lighting. This not only saves energy but also creates an inviting atmosphere.

- **Harvesting rainwater:** Collecting rainwater from rooftops for various purposes like irrigation or even consumption is a sustainable practice that reduces water usage and costs. Adding gutters, downspouts, and storage tanks to your shelter allows you to easily harness this natural resource.

By incorporating these simple yet effective strategies into your DIY shelter construction project, you can unleash creativity while making an environmental impact.

DIY Shelter Projects for Urban Environments: Maximizing Limited Space

Small-Scale Vegetable Garden

Utilize limited space by constructing a small-scale vegetable garden on your urban shelter's roof or balcony. Start by selecting shallow containers and filling them with nutrient-rich soil. Choose compact vegetables that thrive in tight spaces, such as cherry tomatoes, salad greens, and herbs like basil or mint.

Place the containers strategically to maximize sunlight exposure throughout the day. Remember to regularly water the plants and provide necessary nutrients for healthy growth. By growing your own vegetables, you not only save money but also have fresh produce right at your fingertips.

Vertical Storage Solutions

Make the most of vertical space in your DIY shelter construction project through creative storage solutions. Utilize shelving units, hanging baskets, or magnetic strips to keep belongings organized and easily accessible without cluttering limited floor space.

Additionally, repurpose household items like shoe organizers for storing small items or using pegboards as versatile wall organizers. These innovative storage ideas will help you optimize every inch of space while maintaining a tidy living environment.

Multi-Purpose Furniture Design

Maximize limited space within an urban shelter by incorporating multi-purpose furniture designs into your DIY construction plans.

Invest in beds with built-in drawers or cabinets underneath for additional storage options. Foldable tables and chairs allow flexibility when entertaining guests, creating more room for various activities during different times of the day.

Consider modular seating arrangements that can be rearranged according to need while providing extra seating during social gatherings. By choosing multi-functional furniture pieces carefully, you can transform a cramped living area into an efficient and multifaceted haven.

Lightweight and Portable: DIY Shelter Solutions for Outdoor Adventures

When embarking on outdoor adventures, it is crucial to have a lightweight and portable shelter that you can easily carry with you. The good news is that constructing your own DIY shelter doesn't mean sacrificing these essential qualities.

One effective solution is using tarps, which are not only lightweight but also versatile. You can use them as the main structure of your shelter, creating a simple A-frame or lean-to design. With some basic knot tying skills, you can secure the tarp to trees or poles, providing instant protection from the elements.

Another option is utilizing materials such as PVC pipes or bamboo to create a frame for your shelter. These materials are lightweight yet sturdy enough to withstand outdoor conditions. By attaching a waterproof tarp or even repurposed plastic sheets onto this framework, you can build a reliable shelter that offers both portability and durability.

Key Points:

- Tarps are an excellent choice for building lightweight shelters due to their versatility.

- Utilizing PVC pipes or bamboo frames provides stability while keeping the weight low.

- By being resourceful with everyday tools and materials like tarps and PVC pipes/bamboo frames, adventurers can construct their own portable shelters without breaking their backs (or budgets).

From Temporary to Permanent: Long-Term DIY Shelter Options

When it comes to constructing a long-term DIY shelter, there are several options to consider. By utilizing everyday materials, you can create a solid structure that will stand the test of time.

1. Concrete Block Shelter

○ Constructing a shelter using concrete blocks offers durability and stability.

○ The blocks can easily be stacked and secured with mortar for added strength.

○ This type of structure provides excellent insulation against extreme weather conditions.

2. Timber Frame Cabin

○ A timber frame cabin is another long-term DIY shelter option that is both sturdy and aesthetically pleasing.

○ By utilizing wood beams and columns, you can create a reliable framework for your shelter.

○ The walls can then be insulated with recycled materials such as straw or old newspapers.

3. Earthbag Dome House

○ For those seeking an eco-friendly option, an earthbag dome house is worth considering.

○ Using bags filled with compacted soil or sand, you can construct a rounded structure that blends into its natural surroundings.

○ This type of shelter requires minimal construction expertise and offers excellent thermal insulation properties.

Going Off-Grid: Sustainable Energy Solutions for DIY Shelters

Building your own shelter can be a creative and fulfilling project. But why stop at just the physical structure? With a little ingenuity, you can also incorporate sustainable energy solutions to power your DIY shelter.

Solar Power

Harnessing the power of the sun is a popular choice for off-grid shelters. Installing solar panels on the roof allows you to generate electricity from sunlight, which can then be stored in batteries for later use. This renewable energy source is clean, quiet, and abundant.

Wind Power

If you're in an area with consistent wind patterns, utilizing wind turbines can be another effective way to generate electricity. These turbines capture kinetic energy from the wind and convert it into electrical energy that can be used to power lights, appliances, and more.

Hydropower

For those near rivers or other bodies of water with flowing currents, hydropower systems offer another sustainable option. By using water turbines or hydrokinetic devices, you can effectively harness the power of moving water to produce electricity.

Incorporating these sustainable energy solutions into your DIY shelter will not only reduce reliance on fossil fuels but also allow you to live more self-sufficiently off-grid. Plus, these eco-friendly options are cost-effective, provide long-term savings on utility bills, and minimize your environmental impact.

Repurposing and Upcycling: Giving New Life to Everyday Materials

Repurposing everyday materials can be a cost-effective way to create a unique shelter. By thinking creatively and seeing the potential in items that might otherwise be discarded, you can transform ordinary objects into functional components for your DIY construction project.

Turning Trash into Treasure

One of the key principles of repurposing is finding new uses for items that would typically end up in the trash. Instead of buying expensive building materials, consider salvaging materials from abandoned buildings or repurposing household items like pallets, old doors, or windows. These items can be transformed into walls, flooring, or even furniture with a little creativity and elbow grease.

Unleashing Your Creative Side

The beauty of upcycling is that it allows you to truly unleash your creative side. Experiment with different techniques and design ideas to give these everyday materials new life. For instance, you could paint old wooden pallets vibrant colors to bring a pop of personality to your shelter's interior or use reclaimed windows as decorative elements while letting natural light flood in.

By repurposing materials and embracing upcycling techniques, you not only reduce waste but also add an element of uniqueness and individuality to your DIY shelter construction project. Get ready to let your imagination run wild!

Inspiring Examples: Showcasing Unique DIY Shelter Designs

Here are a few inspiring examples of DIY shelter designs that demonstrate the creativity unleashed when using everyday materials:

1. **Pallet Cabin**: One innovative DIY shelter design involves repurposing wooden pallets to create a charming and cost-effective cabin. By assembling pallets into walls, floors, and even furniture, individuals can construct a cozy space for retreat or storage.

2. **Tire House**: Another noteworthy example is the tire house concept, which transforms discarded tires into sturdy building blocks. Stacked vertically and secured with concrete or mortar, these tires form robust walls that offer excellent insulation properties.

3. **Mosaic Bottle Wall**: A visually stunning choice is the mosaic bottle wall technique that uses recycled glass bottles as decorative elements in an eco-friendly shelter design. This method involves embedding bottles within cement structures to create colorful patterns while allowing natural light to filter through.

These unique DIY shelter designs prove that with some imagination and resourcefulness, ordinary materials can be transformed into extraordinary structures - all while making use of sustainable alternatives for construction projects.

Overcoming Challenges: Tips and Tricks for Successful DIY Shelter Construction

1. Plan and Research

Before starting any DIY shelter construction project, it is essential to thoroughly plan and research. This includes understanding the environment in which the shelter will be built, considering local building codes and regulations, and determining the materials needed. Proper planning can help identify potential challenges that may arise during construction and allow for effective problem-solving.

2. Start with a Solid Foundation

The foundation is crucial for the stability of any shelter. Ensuring a strong base will help withstand external forces such as wind, rain, or even earthquakes. It is advisable to invest time building a solid and level foundation using concrete or other appropriate materials.

3. Use Everyday Materials Creatively

To optimize creativity while constructing a DIY shelter, think outside the box when it comes to materials. Repurpose items like pallets, shipping containers, or reclaimed wood to save costs and minimize waste.

4. Consider Weather Conditions

When designing your DIY shelter, take into account the prevalent weather conditions in your area. For instance, if heavy rainfall is common year-round in your location, prioritize waterproofing techniques such as installing proper roofing materials or sealing windows tightly.

5.. Stay Safe Throughout Construction

Safety should always be a priority during DIY projects of any kind; shelters are no exception. Take necessary precautions by wearing protective gear like gloves, safety glasses, and hard hats when using power tools or handling heavy objects.

Successfully completing a DIY shelter construction project requires careful planning, resilience, and creative problem-solving skills.Be prepared to face challenges along the way, but remember that overcoming them can lead to an even more rewarding finished product

Unleashing Your Inner Architect: Encouraging Creativity in Shelter Design

Foster a sense of imagination

Encourage individuals to think outside the box and unleash their creativity when designing shelters. By challenging conventional design norms, unique and innovative solutions can be found using everyday materials. Inspire individuals to imagine what is possible rather than limiting themselves to what is traditional or expected.

Emphasize resourcefulness

Highlight the importance of utilizing readily available materials in shelter construction. Encourage individuals to repurpose items that might otherwise be discarded, such as reclaimed wood or salvaged windows. By embracing resourcefulness, new possibilities emerge, allowing for more sustainable and affordable shelter design options.

Promote collaboration

Foster an environment where collaboration is encouraged among DIY shelter builders. Collaborating with others brings together various skills, perspectives, and ideas that can lead to more creative designs. Creating opportunities for knowledge sharing and brainstorming sessions can ignite fresh inspiration and generate out-of-the-box solutions.

Provide guidance and support

Offer guidance on basic architectural principles without overwhelming beginners with technical jargon. Providing simple instructions and step-by-step tutorials allows individuals to feel empowered in their ability to create functional structures while ensuring safety remains a priority.

By nurturing imagination, promoting resourcefulness, encouraging collaboration, and providing guidance, anyone can become an architect of their own DIY shelter creation using everyday materials. Let your inner architect shine!

Preparing for the Unexpected: An In-Depth Exploration of Prepper Bunkers

In a world filled with uncertainty and unforeseen events, the need for preparedness has become increasingly vital. As individuals seek to protect themselves and their loved ones in times of crisis, prepper bunkers have emerged as a popular solution. These fortified underground shelters offer unparalleled security and self-sufficiency during catastrophic scenarios, providing peace of mind amidst chaos. In this insightful article, we delve deep into the realm of prepper bunkers, delving into their construction methods, essentials supplies required within them, and most importantly, how they aid in safeguarding lives during unexpected emergencies. Join us on an exploratory journey where we uncover the intricacies of these remarkable havens for those who prioritize readiness above all else.

Understanding the Need for Prepper Bunkers

The Importance of Prepper Bunkers

Prepper bunkers are vital for those who prioritize safety and preparedness in the face of unexpected events. These concrete shelters provide a secure haven during natural disasters, pandemics, or societal unrest. With their reinforced walls and sturdy construction, prepper bunkers offer protection against external threats like tornadoes, hurricanes, or even terrorist attacks.

Security and Peace of Mind

When disaster strikes, having a prepper bunker can offer peace of mind knowing that you have a safe space to retreat to. Equipped with essential supplies such as food storage, water purification systems, and medical provisions, these underground sanctuaries ensure your survival needs are met. Moreover, prepper bunkers often come with integrated communication systems that allow contact with the outside world if radio networks fail or cell towers go down.

Self-Sufficiency in Challenging Times

In times of crisis where resources become scarce or supply chains break down, prepping bunkers empower individuals to be self-sufficient. These well-stocked shelters enable occupants to ride out unpredictable situations while minimizing reliance on external support. By providing a long-term storage solution for necessities like non-perishable food items and emergency equipment, prepper bunkers guarantee sustenance and security until the situation stabilizes.

Extra Layer of Protection

Preppers understand the value of being proactive rather than reactive when it comes to safeguarding their loved ones. Prepper bunkers provide an additional layer of protection beyond traditional home security measures by acting as fortified fortresses against both man-made and natural threats. Whether it's civil unrest or severe weather conditions such as tornados or earthquakes, these underground shelters grant families an increased chance at surviving unforeseen circumstances unscathed.

Conclusion

By investing in a prepper bunker, individuals prioritize preparedness over uncertainty when facing potential crises. These underground structures offer not only security but also self-sufficiency during challenging times. With their reinforced walls, essential supplies, and integrated communication systems, prepper bunkers provide a reliable sanctuary where occupants can weather the storm while maintaining peace of mind.

Types of Prepper Bunkers: A Comprehensive Overview

Types of Prepper Bunkers

Underground Bunkers

Underground bunkers are the most popular type of prepper bunkers due to their ability to provide maximum protection against various disasters. Built beneath the ground, these bunkers can withstand natural calamities like earthquakes and protect individuals from nuclear fallout. They are constructed with reinforced steel or concrete walls that offer excellent shielding properties. Some underground bunkers also come equipped with air filtration systems, food storage facilities, and renewable energy sources.

Above-Ground Bunkers

Unlike underground bunkers, above-ground bunkers are situated on the surface level. These structures may resemble small cabins or sheds and can be easily accessed in times of emergency. While they may not provide as much protection as their underground counterparts, above-ground bunkers still offer shelter against severe weather conditions.

Location, Location, Location: Choosing the Ideal Spot for Your Bunker

Choosing the Ideal Spot for Your Bunker

When it comes to selecting a location for your bunker, careful consideration is essential. Here are some key factors to keep in mind:

1. Accessibility: Opt for a spot that is easily accessible, but not too close to major roads or populated areas, as they may become hazardous during times of crisis.
2. Geographical Features: Look for elevated ground and avoid low-lying areas prone to flooding or other natural disasters.
3. Proximity to Resources: Ensure your chosen location has access to fresh water sources and fertile land for sustainable food production.
4. Security and Concealment: Find an area concealed from prying eyes with natural barriers like trees or hillsides that can provide additional cover.

Remember, finding the perfect spot requires diligent research and planning. It's crucial to weigh these considerations against one another before making your final decision on the ideal location for your prepper bunker.

More Resources For further guidance on choosing the right site for your bunker:

- [Article] "Top 10 Considerations When Selecting a Prepper Bunker Location" - offers expert advice on what factors you should prioritize in order of importance.

- [Video] "Exploring Different Types of Bunker Locations" - provides visual examples of potential sites along with pros and cons associated with each option.

Building a Prepper Bunker: Construction Techniques and Considerations

Construction Techniques and Considerations

When it comes to constructing a prepper bunker, there are several techniques and considerations to keep in mind.

Location is Key

First and foremost, the location of your bunker is crucial. It should be situated away from highly populated areas, potential flood zones, and any hazardous materials that could pose a threat. A remote spot with easy access to resources like water and food is ideal.

Materials Matter

Choosing the right materials for your bunker is vital for its longevity and functionality. Reinforced concrete offers excellent durability against natural disasters such as earthquakes or hurricanes. Additionally, thick steel doors can provide added protection against intruders or debris.

Ventilation and Escape Routes

Proper ventilation within the bunker is essential to ensure clean air supply while maintaining stealth. Installing an efficient ventilation system that filters out impurities while preventing external contamination is a must. Moreover, incorporating multiple escape routes allows occupants to evacuate safely in case of emergencies or threats.

Building a prepper bunker requires careful planning and attention to detail. By considering factors such as location, materials, ventilation, and escape routes, you can create a secure refuge that will help you weather unexpected situations with peace of mind.

The Anatomy of a Prepper Bunker: Essential Features and Design Elements

Essential Features of a Prepper Bunker

When designing a prepper bunker, there are several essential features that must be considered. These features include:

1. **Structural Strength**: A prepper bunker should be built with sturdy materials and reinforced walls to withstand intense pressures and potential exterior threats.
2. **Secure Entrances**: The entrance to the bunker should have multiple layers of security, such as heavy-duty doors, biometric locks, and keypad access systems, to prevent unauthorized access.
3. **Ventilation Systems**: Proper ventilation is crucial for ensuring a continuous supply of fresh air inside the bunker while also maintaining a safe environment free from harmful gases or pathogens.
4. **Self-Sustaining Power**: To ensure long-term functionality during emergencies, a reliable power supply system is vital. This can include solar panels, wind turbines, or backup generators.
5. **Water Filtration System**: Access to clean drinking water is essential for survival. A prepper bunker should have an efficient water filtration system in place to purify any available water sources.

Design Elements for Prepper Bunkers

Considerations in the design of prepper bunkers include:

1. **Space Utilization**: Optimal use of space ensures maximum

storage capacity for food supplies, medical equipment, and other essential items required during an emergency situation.

2. **Communication Abilities**: Incorporating communication devices like radios or satellite phones facilitates contact with the outside world even when traditional modes fail.

3. **Sanitation Facilities**: Provision for basic sanitation needs within the bunker safeguards health and hygiene during extended stays underground.

4. **Emergency Exit Routes:** Multiple well-marked exit routes allow quick evacuation if necessary while mitigating any risk of being trapped inside the bunker due to structural damage or infiltration by external forces.

Ventilation Systems: Ensuring Fresh Air Supply in Underground Shelters

Proper ventilation is crucial for the survival and well-being of individuals in underground shelters. Without a constant supply of fresh air, occupants can suffer from carbon dioxide buildup, decreased oxygen levels, and increased humidity—leading to discomfort and even serious health issues. To prevent this, prepper bunkers must be equipped with efficient ventilation systems that circulate air effectively while maintaining security.

The Importance of Air Quality

Maintaining good air quality is essential to sustain life within an underground shelter. Adequate ventilation not only ensures a continuous supply of fresh oxygen but also removes stale air contaminated by exhaled carbon dioxide and other pollutants. This prevents the build-up of harmful gases that could lead to asphyxiation or impaired cognitive function.

Effective Ventilation Systems

To achieve optimal air circulation, underground shelters should rely on mechanical ventilation systems equipped with filters capable of purifying incoming air. These systems help keep out dust particles, allergens, and potentially hazardous substances present outside the shelter while promoting proper airflow indoors.

In addition to mechanical systems, natural forms of ventilation such as windows or vents can also play a role when it's safe to open them without compromising security. By combining these approaches strategically, preppers can ensure a continuous flow of fresh air while minimizing external risks that may arise during crisis situations.

By investing time and resources into developing robust ventilation systems for their bunkers, preppers can improve their chances of surviving unforeseen events without sacrificing comfort or well-being due to inadequate airflow.

Powering Up: Exploring Energy Sources for Prepper Bunkers

In times of crisis, a reliable and sustainable energy source becomes essential for survival. Here are a few options to consider when powering up your prepper bunker:

1. Solar power: Harnessing the sun's energy through solar panels is an excellent choice for long-term sustainability. These panels convert sunlight into electricity, which can be stored in batteries or used directly to power appliances and lighting within the bunker.
2. Wind turbines: If you live in an area with consistent wind patterns, installing a wind turbine could provide a steady source of renewable energy. As the wind spins the turbine blades, it generates electricity that can be stored in batteries or used immediately.
3. Backup generators: While not as sustainable as solar or wind power, having backup generators can ensure a continuous supply of electricity during emergencies. These machines run on fuel sources such as propane or gasoline and come in various sizes to suit different power needs.

Remember that diversifying your energy sources is key to ensuring uninterrupted power supply during unpredictable scenarios. Consider combining multiple sources so that even if one fails, you still have other options available for keeping your prepper bunker fully powered and functioning efficiently.

Water Supply and Purification: Securing the Lifeline Underground

Having a reliable water supply is crucial when preparing for unpredictable situations. In an underground bunker, it becomes even more paramount to ensure access to clean water. Here are some key considerations for securing your water lifeline:

1. **Water Storage:** Stock up on containers that can hold large quantities of water, such as food-grade barrels or heavy-duty plastic jugs. Aim to have at least one gallon of water per person per day for drinking and sanitation needs.
2. **Filtration Systems:** Invest in high-quality filtration systems designed to remove contaminants from various sources of water, including rivers, lakes, and rainwater catchment systems.
3. **Water Purification Tablets:** Including a supply of water purification tablets in your emergency kit is essential for treating questionable or untreated water sources. These convenient tablets can kill harmful bacteria and viruses, making the water safe to drink.

Remember that regular maintenance and monitoring of your stored water supply is crucial to ensure its cleanliness over time.

Stocking Up: Essential Supplies for Long-term Survival

When it comes to stocking your prepper bunker, there are a few key supplies that you can't afford to overlook. Here's a list of essentials:

1. **Water**: Ensure you have enough water stored for each person in your group, with an average of one gallon per day being the recommended amount.
2. **Food**: Build up a stockpile of non-perishable food items such as canned goods, dried grains and beans, and freeze-dried meals.
3. **Medical supplies**: Have a comprehensive first aid kit on hand that includes bandages, medications, and any necessary prescription drugs.

It's important to think ahead and prepare for all potential scenarios when gathering supplies for your prepper bunker. Remember: survival depends on careful planning and having the right provisions at hand.

Food Storage and Preservation: Strategies for Sustenance

When it comes to prepping, having an adequate supply of food is essential. After all, in a disaster scenario, access to grocery stores may be limited or nonexistent. That's why it's crucial to have a solid plan in place for food storage and preservation. Here are some strategies that can help:

1. Stockpile non-perishable items: Start by storing canned goods, dry pasta, rice, beans, and other foods with long shelf lives. These items will provide sustenance during the early stages of a crisis when fresh produce might not be available.
2. Preserve perishables through canning or freezing: If you're fortunate enough to have access to fresh fruits and vegetables, preserving them is a smart move. Canning or freezing these items allows you to extend their lifespan significantly.
3. Rotate your stock regularly: To ensure the freshness of your supplies, maintain a system of rotation where newer products are placed at the back while older ones are used first. This way, you'll avoid wasting food due to expiration dates.

By employing these food storage and preservation strategies as part of your overall bunker plan, you'll increase your chances of staying well-fed during any unforeseen event—an essential aspect of being fully prepared.

Medical Preparedness: Equipping Your Bunker for Health Emergencies

When it comes to health emergencies in your bunker, preparedness is key. Here are some essential steps to equip your bunker for any medical situation that may arise:

1. **Stock up on medical supplies**: Make sure you have a well-stocked first aid kit with bandages, antiseptics, pain relievers, and other basic medical necessities. Additionally, consider storing antibiotics and other prescription medications that may be necessary in an emergency.
2. **Create a makeshift infirmary**: Designate an area of your bunker as a space for treating the sick or injured. Keep it clean and organized with basic equipment such as gloves, masks, thermometers, and blood pressure monitors.
3. **Educate yourself**: Take the time to learn about basic first aid techniques so you can effectively handle minor injuries or illnesses while waiting for professional help. Consider taking courses in CPR and advanced life support to further enhance your skills.

Remember that being prepared goes beyond physical supplies; mental well-being is also crucial during emergencies. Encourage open communication amongst bunker inhabitants to address any concerns or fears related to health issues and potential emergencies. Stay vigilant by regularly checking expiration dates on medicines and updating your knowledge of proper medical procedures through continuous learning opportunities either online or through local training resources.

Preparedness Checklist:

- First aid kit stocked with essentials

- Prescription medications stored

- Designated infirmary area

- Basic medical equipment (gloves, masks, thermometers)

- Knowledge of first aid techniques

- Open communication within the group

Communication Systems: Staying Connected in Isolation

When preparing for isolation or emergencies, it is crucial to have reliable communication systems in place. Losing connection with the outside world can be dangerous and isolating, making it essential to prioritize staying connected even when isolated underground.

Here are some key considerations when planning your bunker's communication systems:

- Satellite phones: Invest in satellite phones as they provide a lifeline during emergencies, functioning even when traditional infrastructure fails.

- Two-way radios: These portable devices allow intra-bunker communication and can also serve as backup means of contact with the outside world.

- Ham radio operators: Connect with local ham radio operators who possess the skills to maintain communication during difficult times.

- Internet access: Consider installing a Wi-Fi network within your bunker linked to an alternative power source such as solar panels or generators.

Remember that effective communication systems ensure timely updates on external situations and allow for coordination of rescue efforts if necessary. By staying connected, you can remain informed and connected despite any unexpected circumstances.

Defending Your Fortress: Security Measures for Prepper Bunkers

Security Measures for Prepper Bunkers

When it comes to defending your fortress, security measures are crucial. Here are a few steps you can take to ensure the safety of your prepper bunker:

1. **Solid Construction**: Start by building your bunker with high-quality materials and reinforce it with steel or concrete walls. These sturdy structures will provide a strong defense against external threats.

2. **Multiple Entry Points**: Consider including multiple entry points in your bunker design. This will allow for alternative escape routes and make it harder for intruders to penetrate the fortification.

3. **Advanced Locking Systems**: Install robust locking systems on all doors and hatches leading into your bunker. Digital locks, biometric scanners, or combination locks can add an extra layer of security and restrict access only to authorized individuals.

4. **Surveillance Equipment**: Implement a reliable surveillance system that includes cameras, motion sensors, and alarm systems both inside and outside the bunker. This will help you monitor any suspicious activity around your perimeter and improve overall situational awareness.

5. **Perimeter Defense:** Secure the area surrounding your prepper bunker by installing fences, barriers, or even landmines if legally permitted in your jurisdiction (remember safety first!). Proper lighting can also serve as a deterrent against potential threats during nighttime.

By implementing these comprehensive security measures alongside other essential preparations like food storage and water purification systems, you'll be better equipped to face whatever unexpected challenges may come your way in times of crisis.

Psychological Preparedness: Maintaining Mental Well-being Underground

While preparing for the unexpected by building prepper bunkers focuses on physical safety, it is equally important to prioritize mental well-being in these underground spaces. Isolation and limited access to natural light can have a profound impact on our mental health, making it crucial to take proactive steps towards maintaining psychological preparedness.

Here are some strategies that can help individuals stay mentally strong while living underground:

1. **Establish routines**: Creating a sense of structure through daily routines can provide comfort and stability during challenging times. Designating specific times for meals, exercise, work or recreational activities helps maintain a sense of normalcy.
2. **Maintain social connections**: Human connection is essential for mental well-being even when living in isolation. Utilize available technology like video calls or internet forums to stay connected with loved ones and support networks outside the bunker.
3. **Prioritize self-care**: It's vital to attend not only to our physical needs but also embrace activities that promote emotional well-being such as reading books, practicing mindfulness or pursuing hobbies that bring joy.

By taking these simple yet effective measures, individuals can bolster their psychological resilience and remain mentally strong while adapting to life underground in preparation for uncertain circumstances ahead.

Preparing Your Mind: A Checklist

- Establish daily routines

- Maintain regular communication with loved ones

- Engage in self-care activities

Maintaining Hygiene and Sanitation in a Bunker Environment

Maintaining Hygiene and Sanitation

In a bunker environment, maintaining proper hygiene and sanitation is crucial for the health and well-being of those living in it. Here are some key steps to follow:

- **Daily Cleaning:** Regularly clean all surfaces with disinfectant wipes or sprays to eliminate germs and bacteria.

- **Proper Waste Disposal:** Establish a system for waste disposal that includes separate bins for recyclables, organic waste, and non-recyclable items. Dispose of waste regularly to prevent odors and potential health hazards.

- **Water Conservation:** Use water efficiently by collecting rainwater or installing water filters to purify available sources. Ensure everyone understands the importance of conserving water.

- **Personal Hygiene Matters:** Encourage good personal hygiene practices such as washing hands frequently, brushing teeth regularly, showering, and changing clothes.

Remember that in a bunker environment, resources may be limited. It's essential to prioritize cleanliness while being mindful of resource conservation. By following these guidelines, you can help create a healthy living space inside your prepper bunker without compromising on sanitation or hygiene standards

Above Ground Preparations: Securing the Perimeter

Securing the Perimeter: Above Ground Preparations

When it comes to preparing for the unexpected, securing the perimeter of your prepper bunker is crucial. Here are a few steps you can take to ensure maximum safety:

1. **Install sturdy fencing**: Start by installing a sturdy fence around your property to deter unwanted visitors. Opt for high-quality materials that can withstand extreme weather conditions.

2. **Set up security cameras**: Invest in a reliable security camera system to monitor all entry points and vulnerable areas around your bunker. Make sure they have night vision capabilities for round-the-clock surveillance.

3. **Implement motion sensors**: Motion sensors are an effective way to detect any unauthorized movement near your bunker. Install them strategically along with bright floodlights to scare off potential intruders.

By taking these above ground preparations seriously, you'll be adding an extra layer of protection to your prepper bunker, ensuring peace of mind during uncertain times.

Family Preparedness: Involving Loved Ones in the Planning Process

Involving Loved Ones in the Planning Process

Preparing for emergencies shouldn't be an individual endeavor. It's crucial to involve your loved ones in the planning process so that everyone is on the same page and can respond effectively when the unexpected strikes.

Here are a few ways to involve your family in emergency preparedness:

- **Communication:** Open lines of communication among family members are vital during emergencies. Discuss potential scenarios, evacuation plans, rendezvous points, and methods of communication.

- **Assign Roles:** Determine specific roles and responsibilities for each person so everyone knows what they need to do during an emergency. This ensures organized coordination and minimizes confusion.

- **Training Sessions:** Conduct regular training sessions with your family members to educate them about essential survival skills such as first aid, fire safety, self-defense, or even basic wilderness knowledge.

- **Emergency Drills:** Regularly practice performing emergency drills with your loved ones. This will help them become familiar with procedures and increase their confidence in responding effectively during an actual emergency situation. By involving your loved ones in this process, you create a sense of unity and reduce anxiety by ensuring that everyone is adequately prepared for any unforeseen circumstances that may arise.

Prepper Bunkers: A Historical Perspective

Throughout history, people have sought ways to protect themselves from unexpected disasters. The concept of prepper bunkers is not new and has been around for centuries. In ancient times, civilizations like the Romans and Greeks built underground tunnels and hideaways as a means of shelter during sieges or wars.

In more recent history, the Cold War era brought a heightened sense of fear regarding nuclear attacks. This led to the construction of numerous fallout shelters by governments and private citizens alike. These bunkers were stocked with supplies such as food, water, medical kits, and even entertainment options to sustain occupants in case of a catastrophic event.

Fast forward to present times, prepper bunkers have evolved with advancements in technology and design. Today's bunkers are often equipped with state-of-the-art ventilation systems, reinforced structures capable of withstanding natural disasters or bombings, and advanced security features that provide peace of mind to those seeking refuge within them.

Whether it is an escalating global conflict or a natural disaster like hurricanes or earthquakes — having a prepper bunker offers people both physical protection from danger and psychological relief from anxiety about what tomorrow may bring. As we delve into the depths of this topic further in this post, we will explore different types of preppers' bunkers available today along with their features and purposes.

Lessons Learned: Real-life Accounts of Bunker Survival

1. Adequate supplies are essential: Survivors who weathered extended periods in bunkers emphasized the significance of stocking up on essential supplies such as food, water, and medical provisions beforehand.

2. Mental well-being matters: Isolation within a bunker can lead to deteriorating mental health; it is crucial to prioritize activities that maintain a positive mindset. Engaging in hobbies, reading books and playing games contributed significantly to emotional stability.

3. Regular maintenance is vital: Neglecting routine upkeep compromised bunker functionality for several survivors. Ensuring proper ventilation systems, power sources, and structural integrity through regular checks will prevent unforeseen issues during emergencies.

4. Communication is key: Establishing reliable communication channels with the outside world facilitates contact with loved ones or emergency responders during isolation situations. Radio transmitters and satellite phones proved invaluable tools for maintaining connectivity.

Budgeting for a Prepper Bunker: Cost Considerations and Alternatives

When it comes to budgeting for a prepper bunker, there are several cost considerations to keep in mind. First and foremost is the location of the bunker. If you choose an underground option, excavation costs can be significant. Additionally, factors like soil composition and groundwater levels may also impact construction costs.

Another key consideration is the size of the bunker. Larger bunkers naturally come with higher price tags due to increased construction materials and labor requirements. It's important to carefully assess your needs and strike a balance between sufficient space and affordability.

While pre-made prepper bunkers can be convenient choices, they tend to be more expensive compared to custom-built options. Building from scratch allows you to control every aspect of the design while potentially saving on costs by utilizing readily available materials or repurposing existing structures.

Ultimately, establishing a realistic budget for your prepper bunker involves weighing these various cost considerations against your preparedness goals, ensuring that you're financially prepared for both short-term expenses and any potential long-term maintenance or renovations required.

Don't miss out!

Visit the website below and you can sign up to receive emails whenever Lloyd Green publishes a new book. There's no charge and no obligation.

https://books2read.com/r/B-A-RYABB-OVMPC

BOOKS 2 READ

Connecting independent readers to independent writers.

Did you love *The Prepper's Ultimate Guide: Building Sustainable Shelters for Long-Term Survival*? Then you should read *Unleashing the Power of TikTok: Discovering Innovative Ways to Generate Income on the Platform*[1] by Coloring Ape!

In today's digital age, social media platforms have become an undeniable force, shaping the way we communicate, entertain ourselves, and even earn a living. Among the multitude of platforms available to users worldwide, TikTok has emerged as a ground-breaking platform that offers unique opportunities for individuals to generate income in innovative and creative ways. With its explosive growth and massive user base, harnessing the power of TikTok has become essential for those looking to capitalize on their talents or business ventures. In this article, we will explore how you can tap into this

---

1. https://books2read.com/u/m2EDpk

2. https://books2read.com/u/m2EDpk

captivating platform's potential and discover groundbreaking methods to unleash your earning potential on TikTok. Join us as we delve into strategies employed by successful influencers and entrepreneurs who have cracked the code to monetizing their content effectively on TikTok – paving the way for a new era of financial success in the ever-evolving realm of social media. Get ready to unlock the limitless possibilities offered by TikTok and transform your passion into profit like never before!

Also by Lloyd Green

The Prepper's Ultimate Guide: Building Sustainable Shelters for
Long-Term Survival
Original Six Era: The Rise of the Chicago Blackhawks Dynasty